RADSPORTS GUIDES

ATV RIDING

TRACY NELSON MAURER

Rourke
Publishing LLC
Vero Beach, Florida 32964

www.rourkepublishing.com

Project Assistance:
The guys at Duluth Lawn & Sport contributed their expertise and enthusiasm...again!

Also, the author extends appreciation to Julie LeMay, Tim Farr, Doug Moon, Mike Maurer, and Kendall and Lois M. Nelson.

Photo Credits:
Cover, page 29: © Pascal Rondeau/Allsport; pages 4, 10, 12, 17, 20, 25, 26, 37, 40, 44: © Adam Campbell Photography; pages 6, 32: courtesy of Bombardier; pages 8, 23, 28, 41: © Curtis Wade/Advanced ATV; pages 18, 39: © Al Bello/Allsport; page 22: © Brian Bahr/Allsport; page 35; © Allsport;

Cover photo: All-Terrain Vehicles, or ATVs, charge down rugged trails in nearly any weather.

Editor: Frank Sloan

Cover and page design: Nicola Stratford

Notice: This book contains information that is true, complete and accurate to the best of our knowledge. However, the author and Rourke Publishing LLC offer all recommendations and suggestions without any guarantees and disclaim all liability incurred in connection with the use of this information.

Safety first! Activities appearing or described in this publication may be dangerous. Take a safety course and use common sense. Always wear safety gear. Even with complete safety gear, risk of injury still exists.

Library of Congress Cataloging-in-Publication Data

Maurer, Tracy, 1965-
  ATV riding / Tracy Nelson Maurer.
     v. cm. — (Radsports guides)
Includes bibliographical references and index.
Contents: All-terrain means all terrain — Mean machines — Stoked to ride — Flying 4x4s — The contest scene.
  ISBN 1-58952-276-1 (hard)
  1. All terrain vehicle racing--Juvenile literature. 2. All terrain vehicle driving--Juvenile literature. [1. All terrain vehicles.] I. Title.
  GV1037 .M27 2002
  796.7—dc21
                              2002008186

Printed in the USA

TABLE OF CONTENTS

ATVs run in every season and over any terrain, including
ice, snow, and, most importantly, mud.

ALL-TERRAIN MEANS ALL TERRAIN

All-Terrain Vehicles, or ATVs, charge over nearly any surface in nearly any weather. Mud, sand, rocks, water, and snow—everything but pavement—make all-terrain action non-stop fun.

ATVs seem like a cross between a motorcycle and a tank. In the 1950s, early ATVs had six fat wheels. The ATVs looked clunky, but some were fast enough to race. A new three-wheel design in the 1970s moved more like a motorcycle. These ATVs were faster than hulky six-wheelers. But three-wheelers tipped over easily. By 1987, the major manufacturers dropped three-wheelers and made four-wheelers instead.

chapter

ONE

BUSY, BUSY, BUSY

About five million people ride ATVs now. Hunters, fishermen, photographers, and campers use four-wheelers to reach remote areas. Hard-core snowmobilers ride ATVs in the off-season. Some 700 government patrols and rescue teams ride ATVs as part of their jobs. Also, many farmers replaced horses and small tractors with ATVs.

ATVs have become the new workhorse for farming, ranching, and general recreation like hunting and back-country travel.

NOW FOR THE SPEED FREAKS

If it's got an engine, a speed freak wants to race it. Riders challenge each other on **quads**, or sport ATVs, in all kinds of races. Stadium supercross races bring the action indoors. A real dirt track carved with jumps, **berms**, and ripples of gnarly bumps called **whoops** push the riders and their machines to the limit. Usually only adults race in the indoor series.

Speed freaks from ages 12 and up race in outdoor motocross races approved by the American Motorcyclist Association (AMA) and the All-Terrain Vehicle Association (ATVA). **Amateurs** test their skills and **endurance** on the rugged dirt tracks. The tracks usually follow a half-mile (800 m) to 1.5-mile (2,400 m) loop.

Quad racers rip around a track.

The Grand National ATV Championships (GNC) series includes outdoor motocross events and Tourist Trophy (TT) events. TT races run on an oval track that includes left and right turns in the infield. The Grand National Cross-Country series (GNCC) races sometimes last for two hours. The ATVA and AMA **sanction** both series to name the best riders in the country.

Grab the leading position at the starting line. Practice your starts!

THE WINNING EDGE

Your machine doesn't win an ATV race. You do. Practice on a track if you can. Drill yourself on your starts. You want the **holeshot,** or the lead position at the start, for a winning edge. Let the other racers eat your dust.

At the starting line-up, put your machine in second gear if your engine can handle it. Watch the flagman closely. Rev up to about half-throttle and hold it a few seconds before the flag or gate drops. Then release the clutch and hammer the throttle.

Another winner's secret? Avoid coasting. Either gas it hard on the straights or brake hard before the turns. Don't slow down behind some snail. Pass! The time you waste behind a slowpoke comes off your finish time.

Pass the slow guy.
Then leave him in the dust.

Fast 4 x 4s

ATVs top out around 80 miles (129 km) per hour. In 2001, an ATV stunt team ran a 1-mile (1.6-km) stretch twice to set an ATV speed record. Although the top speed was 104 miles (167 km) per hour, the Guinness Book of World Records averaged the two runs for an official record of 99.27 miles (159 km) per hour. Passenger Matthew Coulter guided Graham Hicks, the pilot, who is deaf and blind. They plan to try for an even faster time!

Learning to master the whoops can help put you ahead of the others.

FLY ON ALL FOURS

Flying your ATV off jumps riles up the fans. But airtime slows you down. Most riders try to stay low unless they can gain distance off a jump or pass another racer. Besides, landing a 400-pound (181-kg) ATV looks easy until you're 10 feet (3 m) up in the air and falling fast.

In a motocross race, you can't avoid whoop sections. Learn to control your ATV on these mini-jumps or you can easily do an endo, or an end-over biff. Mastering whoops can also help you win a race.

ATTACK THOSE WHOOPS

Practice, practice, practice! Start small and slow. Before you hit the first bump, move your body into a crouched attack position. Bend your knees and hold your elbows out. Shift your weight back. Stay steady on the throttle to avoid an endo.

Follow a straight line through the whoops for steady **momentum**. Some whoops use evenly spaced bumps that flow with rhythm. Staggered bumps knock you around. Practice both kinds.

Add speed each time you pass over your practice whoops. Try to skim the tops instead of dipping into each one.

Plan your corner with the fastest line that lets you pass or block another racer.

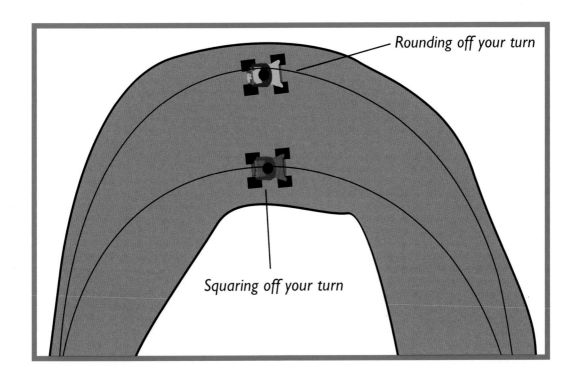

Rounding off your turn

Squaring off your turn

WINNER'S CIRCLE CORNERING

Good cornering helps to put you into the winner's circle. Always brake when you're moving straight ahead, not when you're turning. (This is true for any vehicle.) Look ahead to plan your route, or line, through the corner.

Your line can either square off or round off. Squaring it off means starting tight inside, moving straight to the outside, and turning sharply back down. Rounding it off means you hang on the outside edge.

PUSH YOUR WEIGHT AROUND

For most motocross tracks, you start a corner crouching off the seat. Push your weight back over the rear wheels. At the actual turn, move your weight forward and to the inside to keep the inside wheels on the ground. Always keep your weight low and try not to hang off too far.

You'll feel the back tires bite into the dirt as you head straight again. Push your weight back, but don't do a wheelie!

13

FIND YOUR CLASS

ATV engines are grouped according to size, measured in cubic centimeters (cc). The engines come in four-stroke and two-stroke models. They use air or liquid cooling systems. Each characteristic affects the balance of speed and power.

ATV races are divided into classes by engine size and sometimes by type. So only 91cc to 200cc air-cooled ATVs might race in a heat, or group. Race organizers also split classes according to age, experience, and male or female riders.

CLASSED BY AGE

Motocross ATV classes follow the industry's safety restrictions for age and engine size.

Age	Engine size
6 to 11	0 to 69cc
12 to 15	70 to 90cc
16 to 40-plus	91cc to unlimited

Adults should always supervise riders under age 16. Race classes for riders under age 16 often require Original Equipment Manufacturer (OEM) or stock ATVs. You can't install operating parts made by a different factory on an OEM machine. Read your race rules carefully!

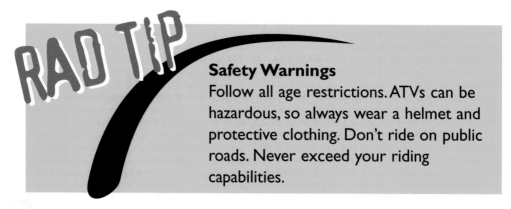

RAD TIP

Safety Warnings
Follow all age restrictions. ATVs can be hazardous, so always wear a helmet and protective clothing. Don't ride on public roads. Never exceed your riding capabilities.

MEAN MACHINES

ATVs come in a full range of sizes from manufacturers such as AlphaSports, Arctic Cat, Bombardier, Cannondale, Honda, Kawasaki, KTM, Suzuki, and Yamaha. If you're under 16, your ATV must be under 90cc. An adult should watch you, too.

chapter

TWO

The right ATV to buy depends on your age, where you ride, and your skill level. You want a lightweight, **agile** ATV for twisty wooded trails or tracks. A heavier, more powerful ATV performs better in open fields and straightaways.

A new machine costs around $5,000. Check the newspaper and sports shops for used ATVs. You might find a deal. If you buy used, check for engine wear. Ask a trusted mechanic to take a look, too.

COOL COOLING SYSTEMS

Air-cooled engines usually cost less than a liquid-cooled engine. They often weigh less and make more noise than liquid-cooled models. Air-cooled engines have fins to catch air. Make sure air can flow across the fins, especially after a few mud bogs. If the engine starts dragging, shut it off. Give it time to cool down.

Generally, a liquid-cooled engine keeps a steady temperature better than an air-cooled engine. But using liquid requires more parts—a radiator, pump, hoses, and **coolant** (also called anti-freeze). More parts add up to more money and more maintenance.

MAKE MAINTENANCE ROUTINE

All winning racers routinely work on their ATVs. Read your owner's manual. Then read it again. Knowing how to fix problems might decide whether you ride home or walk.

The owner's manual usually includes a pre-ride check list. Tape it to your garage wall. Use it every time you ride! Check, lube, and adjust the chain. Look at the air filter—if your motor sucks in dirt, it gags. Add air to the tires and top off the gas tank, too.

Some engines use a special mix of oil and gasoline. Even if you're too young to handle gas, know the mix—just in case the adult doesn't. Most two-stroke engines use 32 parts gas to one part oil, a **ratio** shown as 32:1. Some engines run 100:1! Use a special measuring cup sold at motor shops. The wrong ratio can fry your engine.

After your ride, spiff up your quad. Hose off the mud. Dry and polish it.

STOCK FIRST, UPGRADE LATER

Stock machines without any retrofits rip just fine. Of course, riders tweak their ATVs with **aftermarket** parts. They buy new exhaust pipes, shock absorbers, porting, reeds…you name it.

Super-modified ATV. Perfect for ripping up sand dunes.

RAD TIP

Trail Trouble
Dead engine? A spark plug or a faulty engine kill switch might be the troublemaker. Check the fuel vent and valve, too. It's easy to bump the valve with your knee.

HELMET

RIDING JERSEY

ELBOW & KNEE PADS

GOGGLES

PADDED GLOVES

HIGH-TOP BOOTS

All ATV riders should wear helmets and eye protection. Most races also require special safety gear.

Many racers replace the original **suspension** system for a better ride on rough tracks at high speeds. If you're going to race, check the rules for your class. You probably will need padded handlebars. Most races also require a tether safety kill switch. If you crash, you pull the switch and kill the motor as you fly off the ATV.

MORE AND MORE GEAR

All riders, not just racers, should wear full-face helmets. It's the law in some states. Most sand-dune areas and other special riding parks require helmets. So do racetracks. Put on goggles or other eye protection, too. Dust, bugs, and branches whip at your eyes during a ride.

Most races also require a plastic chest protector, long-sleeve jersey, gloves, and above-the-ankle boots. Racers often wear protective pants, called leathers. Never ride in shorts or short sleeves.

Many people buy a trailer to haul ATVs for family trips. You can also load an ATV into a pick-up truck. A sturdy ramp set helps to move it up and down from the vehicle.

RAD TIP

Lock Down
Thieves steal ATVs. Don't risk it. Bolt a wheel disc brake lock onto the front or rear disc brakes. Or, loop a chain or cable through your ATV and another quad.

RIDE ON THE RIGHT SIDE OF THE LAW

Check with a local dealer, police, or the Department of Natural Resources for your state about registering your ATV. Ask about the next safety training program, too. Most states require drivers under age 16 to complete a safety course. You might also have to carry proof that you passed the course.

The ATV Safety Institute (ASI) offers a program that teaches drivers how to start, stop, handle a hill, and ride over **obstacles**. The training also covers where to ride, safety gear, and the laws you need to know. Even if you're older than 16, finishing a safety course could save you some fines or jail time.

THE QUAD RIDERS' CODE

1. Ride responsibly and put safety first.
2. Take a safety training course.
3. Ride with a buddy.
4. Wear a helmet. No excuses.
5. Wear eye and body protection.
6. Enforce the "one ATV, one person" rule.
7. Stay on the trail or riding area.
8. Respect other people and the land.
9. Promote a better image for the ATV sport.

Protect your body with the right gear.

Ride alert everywhere you go. Crashes with trains, cars, cliffs, fences, trees, rocks, and animals often end in pain—or worse. Use common sense and common courtesy. Put your brain in gear when you rev that engine.

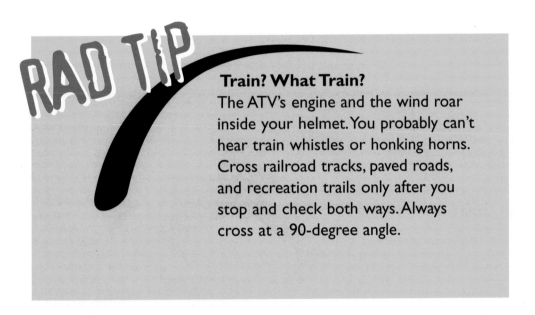

RAD TIP

Train? What Train?
The ATV's engine and the wind roar inside your helmet. You probably can't hear train whistles or honking horns. Cross railroad tracks, paved roads, and recreation trails only after you stop and check both ways. Always cross at a 90-degree angle.

SHAPE-UP

Your body takes a pounding when you ride an ATV. Before you hop onto your quad, warm up for ten minutes with an easy jog. Never stretch cold muscles. After your ride, stretch your neck, arms, torso, and legs. Hold each stretch for 60 seconds. Stretching after a session beats sore, achy muscles later.

Build your strength, balance, and endurance with a regular exercise routine. Lift weights. Do sit-ups and push-ups (zillions and zillions). Lunges and squats build power and endurance in your **quadriceps**, or thighs, too.

Cross-train with personal watercraft riding, mountain biking, or in-line skating. Eat healthy foods. Keeping fit helps you to control your ATV better, even during long sessions.

Mountain biking is excellent cross-training for ATV riders.
It helps build muscle strength and endurance.

STOKED TO RIDE

ATV riding amps up your **adrenaline**. Riding also comes with **responsibilities**. You're operating a motor vehicle. Just like a driver in a car, you need to follow the rules of the road. Signal your turns:

- Left turn: left arm extended straight out
- Right turn: left arm out, forearm raised, with elbow at 90-degree angle
- Stop: left arm raised straight up
- Slow: left arm out and angled toward ground

Keep some space between you and the rider ahead of you, too. If you're within 100 feet (30.5 m) of a walker, snowmobile, or motorcycle, slow down to 10 miles (16 km) per hour. Every person, animal, and vehicle has the right of way.

chapter

THREE

FLY ON ALL FOURS

Accidents happen. Engines die. Storms drop in. Ride ready for anything. Check the weather forecast before you go, especially in the mountains. Dress in layers under your protective gear. Avoid cotton next to your skin. Fabrics that wick moisture away from your skin keep you warm and comfortable.

RAD TIP

Pack for the ride
Here are a few packing suggestions:
- A copy of your owner's manual
- Towrope
- New spark plugs and a compact electrical connection tester
- Small toolkit with a wrench, pliers, screwdriver, chain breaker, and extra chain links
- Multi-purpose tool with a knife, like a Leatherman
- Tire pressure gauge and tire repair plug kit
- First-aid kit
- Flashlight
- Map and compass
- Charged cell phone

STICK YOUR STANCE

ATVs require you to shift your weight from side to side, backward and forward. You don't sit still. Start with the right **stance** to improve your control as you move around.

Keep your head and eyes up. Look ahead and stay alert. Relax your shoulders and bend your elbows out slightly as you grab the handlebars. Tuck your knees in a bit by the gas tank and plant your feet on the footrest.

A low and centered stance with knees bent gives the rider more control over rough terrain.

Crash Course

Bad biff? Stay calm. If you feel woozy or sick, or if bones are sticking out where they usually stay in, call 911 or go to the emergency room. If you're not hurt, check your ATV for damage. Adjust your handlebar, test the air pressure in the tires, and make sure the brakes still work. Then ride!

When going up or down hills, shift your weight to keep your machine stable.

SHIFT THAT BODY

Your stance and speed change with the terrain. Lean your body uphill when you ride across slightly sloped terrain. Also keep some weight on the low-side peg. It helps the tires dig in. Sometimes turning the front wheels slightly uphill gains **traction**, too.

Most ATVs climb hills easily. They can climb until they're so vertical that they flip over. Adult riders should stick to hills with slopes less than 25 degrees. Kids should climb hills with slopes less than 15 degrees. Start small.

KING OF THE HILL

Check out the hill first. Decide on a straight line up the hill. Don't plan to swerve around boulders or trees. If you can't find a good route up, forget it. Go around.

As you climb a hill, shift your body weight forward over the handlebars. Crouch with your feet planted in the footrests. Stay in a low gear and move forward with a steady pace. Jerky starts and stalls can knock you backward.

Go down a hill following a straight line, too. Move your weight back. Never coast downhill in neutral. Keep it in the lowest gear. Brake gently so the brakes don't lock up. Give the right of way to a driver coming up the hill.

27

ROCK TO ROLL

Deep mud holes beg for you to splash through them. Downshift to first. A steady forward crawl avoids spinning the tires. If you start to feel sticky, stay on the throttle and stand up. Rock from side to side. When the tires grab hold, add weight to those tires before they spin. Spinning tires dig a deeper hole. If you're stuck, give up. Get out that trusty towrope and ask your buddy for help.

Keep the air intake out of the mud. Shift your weight back and try to point the nose up. Even when your ATV starts to float, jazz the throttle to clear the hoses. Wiggle the handlebars to help the tires find traction.

If the engine drowns, turn off the motor before the water damages anything. Float your ATV to shore and let the water drain out. Dry the air filter. Change the spark plugs and check the oil.

MORE PLACES TO RIDE

Explore new places to ride. Escape the snow during the winter and try the Imperial Sand Dunes or other designated dune riding areas in California. The smooth sand terrain there lets you try moves that are too risky other places.

Mountain riding stokes ATV riders, too. The steep, winding trails—or lack of them—challenges even the best riders. Give yourself time, at least six hours, to adjust to the higher elevation.

Sand dunes add to your ATV riding skills. The smooth terrain creates a soft landing for big-air moves.

28

Clear Your Clearance
Know how much ground clearance you have. Some owners put on oversize tires and a lifter kit to add height. Top off the air in your tires, too. General mud riding takes about 3 to 4 pounds per square inch (psi).

Special air filters on the front of your ATV will help protect your engine from mud and sand.

INVITATION ONLY RIDING

Ride where you're invited. Stay on marked trails. Stay off public roads. Private landowners take back access rights when ATVs stray into their pastures, gardens, and lawns.

Don't chase animals with your ATV or run down innocent trees. Trashing the trails ruins the sport for everyone.

Join a local ATV club to find the best riding areas and hook up with fun-runs, scrambles, races, and other events. Check with the National Off-Highway Vehicle Conservation Council, or NOHVCC, for the clubs near you. The NOHVCC promotes safe riding and works to keep trails open to ATVs.

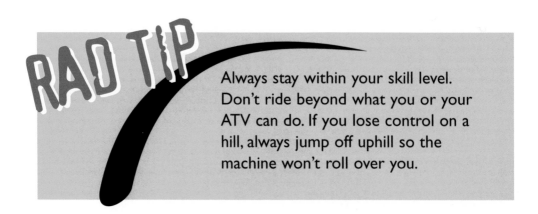

RAD TIP

Always stay within your skill level. Don't ride beyond what you or your ATV can do. If you lose control on a hill, always jump off uphill so the machine won't roll over you.

FLYING 4 X 4s

An ATV is not a toy. Manufacturers build their vehicles to perform safely under certain conditions.

Your owner's manual probably says that you should NEVER DO WHEELIES, JUMPS, OR STUNTS on your ATV. Yep. **Freestyle** riding is EXTREMELY DANGEROUS. It makes the old-schoolers angry. They think freestyle ruins the sport's reputation. Don't let it.

chapter

FOUR

DANCING RHINOS

Freestyle ATVs look like dancing rhinos. Riders try to pull smooth, stylish, and very sick tricks. Only highly skilled riders, or pilots, command these four-wheel beasts. ATVs are much more difficult to control in the air than two-wheel motorcycles.

Freestyle and racing ATVs have heavy-duty suspensions on the front and rear of the machine. This allows the rider to have better control over rough terrain.

Think of the long pole tightrope walkers use for balance. You use the handlebar as a balancing pole. On a motorcycle, the handlebar positions your hands far out on each side of the front tire. On an ATV, the handlebar doesn't stretch past the tires. It's a short balancing lever. You must use more force to balance the ATV.

BROKE AND BROKEN

A few ATV pilots have mastered some freestyle motocross tricks. These dudes practice, and practice, and practice. When you see freestylers, remember that they don't drive beater ATVs. They modify their rides with better suspension, lifters, engine upgrades, and other tweaks. Cha-ching!

Along the way, they break a lot of those fancy ATV parts, too. They also break a lot of their bones, teeth, and other body parts. Freestyling is not cheap and it's not painless.

If you think you're ready to notch it up to freestyling, check your tires, wheels, shocks, and suspension. Absolutely fine-tune everything. Also make sure your helmet, goggles, boots, gloves, and chest protector can handle the beating.

RAD TIP

Air Check
During a wheelie or on straightaways, your quad might pull to the left or right. Check your air pressure in the tires.

RADTRICK: SINGLE JUMPS

Insanity Level: 1 out of 10

Serious motocross and supercross racers master jumps to win. Once you dial in your jumps, you can think about freestyle tricks.

Always scope out the landing zone before you jump. If it's a blind jump, meaning you can't see the landing zone from the ramp, ask your buddy to stay on the landing side. Your buddy should signal when it's safe to jump.

Start small. Look for a smooth ramp. You don't need a big lip or a sloped landing zone. Crouch into an attack position. Bend your knees and keep your elbows out. Stay steady on the gas up the ramp.

In the air, you might need to blip the throttle to help keep the front-end up. You want to land on your rear wheels. Landing flat on all fours feels worse than a belly flop into the shallow end of the pool. Ouch!

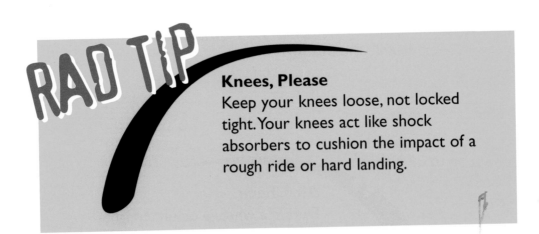

Knees, Please
Keep your knees loose, not locked tight. Your knees act like shock absorbers to cushion the impact of a rough ride or hard landing.

On a single jump, try to land the rear wheels first. Nose-first landings often fling you over the handlebar.

RADTRICK: DOUBLE JUMPS

Insanity Level: 4 out of 10

Racers use front-wheel landings off jumps to stay on the gas for the next jump. Double jumps require nose-first landings. To lower your front wheels in the air, tap the rear brake or push down on the handlebars. If the nose dips too far, rev the throttle all the way as you shift your weight back slightly.

A double jump usually uses a launch ramp and a landing ramp followed by another set of ramps. Practice on a tabletop jump first. A tabletop also has up-and-down ramps, but with a level surface between them. You can land short without biffing. Dial in your timing. Aim at the base of the next jump.

Add more speed as you practice. Move from the tabletop to your first double jump only when you really feel ready.

RAD TIP

Don't hit a jump sitting. Extra weight on the back tires compresses the shocks. The ATV becomes a slingshot, flinging you off.

Landing a large double jump requires you to tip the front of your ATV down.

Dial in your basic wheelies. Then go for a one-wheeled wheelie. Expect to dig dirt often as you practice that one! (Also expect to wear out your clutch.)

RADTRICK: WHEELIE

Insanity Level: 2 out of 10

Wheelies look cool. They also come in handy on the trail. You work wheelies differently on a manual-clutch ATV than on an auto-clutch ATV.

On a manual-clutch quad, you pull in the clutch and shift into first or second. Rev the throttle past halfway. Then shift your weight back and pop the clutch. You want to hang in the air at your balance point. Blip the throttle to raise the nose. Tap the rear brake to bring the nose down. Sometimes just pushing or pulling the handlebar with your arms can keep the ATV balanced.

For an auto-clutch ATV, press down the foot shifter. Rev to about half throttle. Then pull up on the handlebars as you check into gear. Rev it way up. Shift your weight back, too. Some people even put a foot on the rear grab-bar.

RADTRICK: DONUTS

Insanity Level: 2 out of 10

Level, open terrain works best for a smooth donut, or ground-level 360 (say three-sixty). Dunes work great and so does soft dirt, called "chocolate cake." Come into the turn at just past half throttle. Crank your handlebars and lean inward. Jazz the throttle. Watch that you don't lean too far inside.

Donuts have no real purpose in racing, but they are still really fun.

One of the most extreme big air tricks is the Superman.

RADTRICK: HEEL CLICKER

Insanity Level: 8 out of 10

WARNING: PROFESSIONALS ONLY, EXTREMELY DANGEROUS

Look for a ramp that gives you decent airtime. Once you're off the lip, kick your feet up and outside your arms. Hold the handlebars as you click your feet together. Then drop your feet back down and take a crouched position for the landing.

RADTRICK: CLIFFHANGER

Insanity Level: 11 out of 10

WARNING: PROFESSIONALS ONLY, EXTREMELY DANGEROUS

You definitely need huge air for this one. Just as you leave the lip, use the energy to push yourself off the seat. Reach up high with your arms. Stretch out your toes to catch the underside of the handlebars. Keep your head up. Then reach down for the handlebars as you kick your feet back into position. Bend your knees for the landing.

THE CONTEST SCENE

Quad freestylers defy gravity. They push **physics** to the brink.
But they don't bring in huge crowds—yet. Most ATV freestyle big-air
contests are sideshows to monster truck rallies, 4 x 4 car or truck
motocross, or quad supercross events. Sometimes you can catch a
late-night quad freestyle show on cable television. Videos sold
through quad magazines or on the Internet also let you check out
the action.

chapter

FIVE

JOIN THE FUN!

Most ATV riders don't become freestyle pilots. Save your money and your body parts for awesome trail rides and maybe motocross racing.

Join the ATVA no matter how you ride. If you want to race in ATVA/AMA motocross events, upgrade to the ATVA Competition Level or become a full AMA member. Keep your receipt! You need to show it at every race until you receive your official membership card. Read the rule book. Twice (at least). You can even download it from the Internet. Every racetrack and club works a bit differently. Ask questions if you don't understand a rule or you're not sure about an event.

BIG-TIME QUAD KINGS (AND QUEENS!)

Freestylers Nate Freese, Travis Cain, and Dana Creech steal the show wherever they go. Fans know them by their outrageous tricks, like double heel clickers and one-handed supermans.

The sport has many big-time racing champions, too. Gary Denton, who recently retired, earned the GNC title eight times during in his legendary career. Four-time Pro Quad Indoor Champion Tim Farr also won the GNC three times. GNC racer Traci Lenig Cecco and many other top riders regularly rip on quad tracks all over the country. Watch for them at a contest near you!

ATV racers share tips and information during events.

FAN FOCUS

Champ Rider
Name: Tim Farr
Birthday: May 7, 1972
Home: Canal Fulton, Ohio
Racing Since: 1989
Pro Since: 1991
Started Out: Earned a Mechanical Engineering degree and worked as a mechanical engineering technician; now his racing career supports him
Titles: 1999, 2000, 20001, 2002 Pro Quad Points Champion
1995, 1996, 1998 GNC Pro Champion
Cross-Trains: Motocross, mountain biking, tennis, racquetball, weight lifting, running

GO PLAY

Ride your ATV. Ride as often as you can. Ride in different places, from wicked wooded trails to monster motocross tracks. Ride in the snow, mud, sand, and rocky hills. Practice your moves. And, most importantly, have fun—safely.

If you want to learn more about ATV riding, visit your library or the Web. Try to catch a live event. Watch ATV videos. You can even play computer and video games about ATV riding. Enjoy the sport any way you can!

Go ride. Have fun. Be safe!

FURTHER READING

ATV Rider Course Handbook from the ATV Safety Institute.

ATV Magazine

Chilton's ATV Handbook (Chilton's General Interest Manuals) by Christopher Bishop. Delmar Learning, 1999.

Dirt Wheels Magazine

The Field & Stream All-Terrain Vehicle Handbook: The Complete Guide to Owning and Maintaining an ATV by Monte Burch. The Lyons Press, 2001.

The Haynes ATV Basics Manual (Techbook series) by Mike Mavrigian, John H. Haynes. Haynes Publishing Company, April 1996.

Off-Road Racing (Fast Tracks series) by A. T. McKenna. Abdo & Daughters, 1998.

WEBSITES TO VISIT

www.ama-cycle.org

www.atvaonline.com

www.atving.com

www.nohvcc.org

atvsafety.org

GLOSSARY

adrenaline (ah DREN ul in) — a body chemical released when the person is startled, afraid, or excited

aftermarket (AF tur MAR kit) — replacement or add-on parts; not the original part

agile (AJ ihl) — quick, lively, responds well

amateurs (AM uh choorz) —athletes who compete for fun; they receive no pay for winning

berms (BURMZ) — banks or mounds of dirt

coolant (KOO lunt) — a solution or gas used to lower the temperature of a system, usually an engine; also called anti-freeze

endurance (en DUHR ans) — ability to keep going

freestyle (FREE stihl) — in ATV riding, adding jumps and tricks to a ride; often this includes using ramps to launch into the air

holeshot (HOHL shot) — the lead position at the start of a race

momentum (moh MEN tum) — forward or ongoing movement

obstacles (AHB stuh kilz) — things blocking a path; in mountain bike riding, these include rocks, logs, and streams

physics (FIZ iks) — the science of matter, energy, motion, and force

quadriceps (KWAD reh seps) — muscles on the top side of the thighs

quads (KWADZ) — sport models of All-Terrain Vehicles (ATVs); also called four-wheelers

ratio (RAY she oh) — the relationship between two numbers or measures; the number of times the first contains the second

responsibilities (reh spon sah BILL ah teez) — duties; tasks that are proper or right to do

sanction (SANGK shun) — to make, approve, or check the rules

stance (STANSE) — the proper body position for control and safety

suspension (suh SPEN shun) — the system of shock absorbers connected to the wheel axles

traction (TRAK shun) — the ability of a foot or wheel to grip the terrain or surface

whoops (HWOOPS) — a series of tightly spaced bumps; also called whoop-de-dos

INDEX

ABOUT THE AUTHOR

Tracy Nelson Maurer specializes in nonfiction and business writing. Her most recently published children's books include the *Radsports I* series, also from Rourke Publishing LLC. She lives with her husband Mike and two children in Superior, Wisconsin.